The Bread Book

Multiplying and Dividing

Tony Hyland

Publishing Credits

Editor
Sara Johnson

Editorial Director
Emily R. Smith, M.A.Ed.

Editor-in-Chief
Sharon Coan, M.S.Ed.

Creative Director
Lee Aucoin

Publisher
Rachelle Cracchiolo, M.S.Ed.

Image Credits

The author and publisher would like to gratefully credit or acknowledge the following for permission to reproduce copyright material: cover, Shutterstock; p.4 The Photo Library/Alamy; p.5 Photo Edit; p.6 Photos.com/Jupiter Images; p.7 (left) Shutterstock; p.7 (right) Shutterstock; p.8 Corbis; p.9 Shutterstock; p.10 Shutterstock; p.12 Bigstock Photos; p.13 Shutterstock; p.14 Bigstock Photos; p.15 Shutterstock; p.16 The Photo Library/Alamy; p.17 Alice McBroom Photography; p.18 (top left) 123rf; p.18 (center) The Photo Library/ Alamy; p.18 (center right) Shutterstock; p.18 (bottom left) Shutterstock; p.18 (right) Shutterstock; p.18 (bottom right) Shutterstock; p.19 The Photo Library/ Alamy; p.20 Shutterstock; p.21 Shutterstock; p.24 (all) Shutterstock; p.25 Shutterstock; p.26 (left) Shutterstock; p.26 (center) Alamy; p.26 (right) The Photo Library/Science Photo Library; p.28 123rf; p.29 123rf.

While every care has been taken to trace and acknowledge copyright, the publishers tender their apologies for any accidental infringement where copyright has proved untraceable. They would be pleased to come to a suitable arrangement with the rightful owner in each case.

Teacher Created Materials

5301 Oceanus Drive
Huntington Beach, CA 92649-1030
http://www.tcmpub.com
ISBN 978-0-7439-0893-1
© 2009 Teacher Created Materials Publishing

Table of Contents

Bread

Bread is one of the world's most important and useful foods. Most people eat some type of bread every day. Today, people can buy bread from stores or from small **bakeries**. Some people even bake bread at home.

Bread Down Under

Each Australian eats an average of 97 pounds (44 kg) of bread every year!

One Slice of Bread

The U.S. government helps its people make healthy food choices. It says that people should eat 3 ounces (85 g) of **whole-grain** food each day.

One slice of whole-wheat bread weighs 1 ounce (28 g). So if you ate 3 slices of whole-wheat bread, this would meet the required 3 ounces needed each day.

LET'S EXPLORE MATH

A sandwich is made up of 2 slices of bread. Use **multiplication** to work out how many slices of bread:

a. make up 18 sandwiches.

b. make up 240 sandwiches.

Now, use **division** to work out how many sandwiches are made from:

c. 96 slices of bread.

d. 158 slices of bread.

Different Shapes and Sizes

Bread is made in many shapes and sizes. Take a look at a loaf of bread. What shape does it remind you of? It is probably shaped like a rectangular **prism**. This shape is great for making sandwiches.

rectangular prism

This whole-wheat loaf has around 16 slices.

This loaf has nuts and seeds in it. It is healthy and tasty.

These bread rolls are shaped like **spheres**. Bread rolls are like really small loaves of bread.

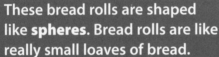

LET'S EXPLORE MATH

One whole-wheat loaf has 16 slices.

a. If a family has 3 loaves of bread and eats 8 slices, how many slices are left?

b. If a bakery has 14 loaves of bread, how many slices of bread do they have?

What Is in Bread?

Flour is a main **ingredient** (in-GREE-dee-uhnt) of bread. Add water, **yeast,** and some salt to the flour. You have made a simple loaf of bread!

Wheat flour is made from ground-up wheat. Long ago, people used stones to **grind** the wheat into flour. Today, the wheat is sent to **mills** and is turned into flour.

A worker at a flour mill

Wonderful Wheat

Wheat is a grain. The head of the wheat has seeds called kernels. The kernels are sent to flour mills. Milling turns the kernels into flour.

Did You Know?

Wheat can be measured in **bushels** (BOO-shelz). One bushel of wheat:

- contains approximately 1 million kernels
- weighs approximately 60 pounds (27 kg)
- can make 42 loaves of white bread
- can make 90 loaves of whole-wheat bread.

LET'S EXPLORE MATH

Fresh Flour Mill supplies flour to 35 bakeries.

a. On Monday, each bakery needs 12 bags of flour. How many total bags does Fresh Flour Mill need to supply?

b. On Tuesday, each bakery needs 22 bags of flour. How many total bags does Fresh Flour Mill need to supply?

The Wheat Farmer

Farmers grow wheat. The wheat is **harvested** (HAR-ves-tuhd). Then it is sent to a flour mill. The wheat grains are broken down and turned into flour. Bakeries buy the flour and make loaves of bread. Many of the loaves of bread are then sold to grocery stores.

Wheat is harvested on a farm.

Let's say a 1 pound (0.5 kg) loaf costs around $1.00. The wheat farmer gets about 5 cents of that $1.00. The graph below shows you where the rest of the money goes.

LET'S EXPLORE MATH

This bar graph shows that a farmer gets $0.05 from 1 loaf of bread. How much would the farmer get for:

a. 12 loaves of bread?   **c.** 45 loaves of bread?

b. 20 loaves of bread?   **d.** 36 loaves of bread?

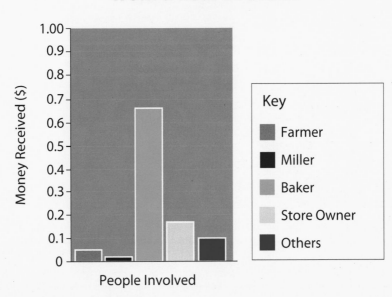

Distribution of Money Made from a Loaf of Bread

Money Received ($)

People Involved

Key
- Farmer
- Miller
- Baker
- Store Owner
- Others

A Closer Look at Flour

What is the difference between whole-wheat bread and white bread? It is the flour.

Whole-wheat Bread

Whole-wheat bread is made from whole-wheat flour. Whole-wheat flour uses 100% of the wheat grain.

wheat grains

white flour

White Bread

White bread is made from wheat flour, too. But the flour used to make white bread is not made from all of the wheat grain. Parts of the wheat grain were taken out at the flour mill when it was turned into flour. White flour uses around ¾ of the wheat grain.

Fiber in Bread

Some types of bread are healthier to eat than others. Whole-wheat breads have more **fiber** in them than white breads.

Look at the different parts of wheat. The bran part is high in fiber. This bran forms part of whole-wheat flour.

germ

endosperm

bran

Bran is found in the outside covering of the wheat grain. The germ is like a seed. It makes new wheat plants grow. The endosperm is used to make white flour.

Bran is not in white flour. It is taken out of the wheat grain at the mill. Whole-wheat bread has 4 times as much fiber as white bread. One slice of whole-wheat bread has ½ of an ounce (14 g) of fiber.

Reading Recipes Right

A baker needs a **recipe** (REH-suh-pee) to make bread. A recipe is a list of ingredients needed to make something. A recipe will also tell you *how* to make something.

But there is more to recipes than just reading them.

A baker makes dough before baking

LET'S EXPLORE MATH

Kim the baker needs to work out halves and quarters of some of his ingredients. First, he needs ½ of 16 cups of flour.

a. Which expression below shows ½ of 16?

$\frac{1}{2} \div 16$ $\qquad$ 2×16 $\qquad$ $\frac{1}{2} \times 16$

b. How much flour does he need to use?

Then, Kim needs ¼ of 24 cups of water.

c. Which expression below shows ¼ of 24?

$\frac{1}{4} \div 24$ $\qquad$ $\frac{1}{4} \times 24$ $\qquad$ 4×24

d. How much water does he need to use?

Bakers need to use math so that their bread turns out just right. Recipes give **measurements** of ingredients. For example, a bread recipe might tell the baker to use 5 and ½ cups of flour.

The measurement "5 and ½ cups of flour" is a mixed number. A mixed number is a whole number and a **fraction**. It means that the bread recipe uses 5 whole cups of flour, plus ½ of a cup of flour.

If the baker could not read the fractions in a recipe, then the bread might not be tasty to eat.

Baking Bread

Here's a simple bread recipe used by bakers. Think about the math needed to make these loaves of bread.

Simple Bread

Makes 2 loaves

Ingredients
- 5 ½ cups bread flour
- 1 tablespoon (T.) salt
- 2 ½ T. rapid rise yeast
- 16 ounces very warm water
- 1 T. olive oil
- 2 T. honey

What to Do

1. Place all dry ingredients in an electric mixer bowl.
2. Pour the warm water into the bowl.
3. Add the oil and the honey. Mix well.
4. Let the dough rest for 10 minutes.
5. Mix again on a higher speed for 3 minutes.

6. Place the dough onto a floured board or table.
7. **Knead** the dough 3 to 4 times.
8. Put the dough back into the mixer bowl and cover with a cloth. Leave in a warm place for 1 hour.
9. After 1 hour, knead the dough again 3 to 4 times.

LET'S EXPLORE MATH

The recipe makes 2 loaves of bread. Let's double the recipe to make 4 loaves of bread. Double means to multiply the number by 2.

a. Double each of the ingredients (page 18).

b. If you cut each loaf of bread into 14 slices, how many slices of bread will you have in all 4 loaves?

10. Split dough into 2 loaves and put into 2 loaf pans.
11. Cover both loaves with cloths. Leave in a warm place to rise for 45 minutes.
12. Preheat the oven to 375°F (190°C) and bake for 30 to 35 minutes.
13. Remove bread from loaf pans. Leave for 30 minutes to cool; then slice and enjoy!

A Baker's Dozen

People often order loaves of bread made by the dozen. Normally, 12 items make a dozen. Around the thirteenth century, bakers began to add an extra loaf to every dozen. They did not want to be accused of cheating the customers. So 13 items has become known as a baker's dozen.

Eat Your Plate!

The trencher was a common kind of bread in the **Middle Ages**. This was a thick, flat piece of bread. It was used as a plate. People ate their meat and vegetables from the trencher. Then they ate the trencher itself. Today, a trencher is a flat wooden platter used for serving food.

Baking a Baker's Dozen

Today, some bakers still bake bread in "baker's dozens." Most baking trays are rectangular in shape. Bakers must work out the best ways to fit 13 loaves or rolls on 1 pan.

Look at this baking tray. It has 13 rolls on it. Let's do the math:

3 + 2 + 3 + 2 + 3 = 13

Here is another way of fitting 13 rolls on a tray:

4 + 5 + 4 = 13

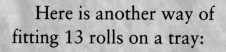

A baker's dozen amounts to 13. Which two expressions below amount to 13? *Hint:* Remember to work out the part in the parentheses (par-ENTH-es-eez) first.

a. (3 × 2) + 3   **c.** (2 × 5) + 3

b. (4 × 3) + 1   **d.** (4 × 5) + 4

Bread Around the World

There are hundreds of different types of bread. No bakery can make all of them! Most bakers choose about a dozen styles of bread. They bake bread that they know customers want to buy. No baker wants to throw out unwanted bread at the end of the day.

Mexican tortilla

French baguette

Indian naan

American cornbread

Bread is popular all around the world. Breads are made from recipes that include flour and water or milk.

Millions of Loaves

In the United Kingdom, around 12 million loaves of bread are bought each day.

LET'S EXPLORE MATH

Often, Mexican tortillas are packed in bundles of 8.

a. How many packets of 8 tortillas would a restaurant owner need to buy if she wanted to serve 60 customers her famous beef and spicy bean tortillas?

b. Would she have any tortillas left over? If so, how many?

Bread Time Line

People have made bread for over 5,000 years. Let's take a look at bread through the centuries.

3000 B.C.	2000 B.C.	1000 B.C.	A.D. 1200	A.D. 1666
Ancient Egyptians made bread from grain. Bread was used to buy things, instead of money.	In India, grain was farmed. Breads were made from the grain.	In Rome, bread made with yeast became popular.	In England, laws were made about the price of bread.	The Great Fire of London might have been started by a baker.

Time in Years

A decade is 10 years of time. A century is 100 years of time. There are 10 decades in a century.

1777

Wheat was first planted in the United States.

1850s

The United States had over 2,000 bakeries. Over 6,700 people worked in them.

1928

A bread-slicing machine was first shown in the United States.

2003

The state of Texas produced enough wheat in this year to make 6.2 billion loaves of bread!

LET'S EXPLORE MATH

Ancient Egyptians were making bread 3,000 years ago. That is 30 × 100 years. Find the missing numbers in the following equations. You will be multiplying or dividing by 10s and 100s.

a. $3,000 \div \underline{\hspace{1cm}} = 30$

b. $20 \times 100 = \underline{\hspace{1cm}}$

c. $52 \times \underline{\hspace{1cm}} = 520$

d. $\underline{\hspace{1cm}} \div 10 = 100$

Counting Cakes

Ada is making cupcakes for a bake sale. Her recipe makes 25 cupcakes in a batch.

Solve It!

a. If Ada wants to sell 150 cupcakes, how many batches will she need to make?

b. Ada wants to sell the cupcakes in trays that hold 4 cupcakes each. How many trays of cupcakes will she be able to sell? Will she have any cupcakes left over?

c. If Ada sells each tray of cakes for $2.00, how much money will she make?

Use these steps to help you solve the problems.

Step 1: Work out how many batches of cupcakes Ada will need to make 150 cupcakes.

Step 2: Work out how many trays of 4 cupcakes Ada will be able to sell.

Step 3: Find out if there are any cupcakes left over. Write the answer with the remainder as a fraction.

Step 4: Work out how much money Ada will make if she sells all her trays of cupcakes.

Glossary

bakeries—stores where bread is cooked and sold

bushels—a measurement of wheat

division—a mathematical operation where a number is grouped into equal parts

fiber—the part of food that your body cannot digest

fraction—part of a group, number, or whole set

grind—crush

harvested—collected from the fields

ingredient—one of the foods needed to make a recipe

knead—to massage into dough

measurements—units of size or quantity

Middle Ages—the period of European history from about A.D. 500–1500

mills—factories for grinding grain

multiplication—a mathematical operation where a number is added to itself many times

prism—a 3-D shape

recipe—instructions for cooking something

spheres—3-D globe shapes

whole-grain—foods made from whole-wheat flour

yeast—a substance used to help bread rise when it is cooking

Index

Let's Explore Math

Page 5:
a. 36 slices   **b.** 480 slices   **c.** 48 sandwiches   **d.** 79 sandwiches

Page 7:
a. 16 × 3 = 48 slices. 48 − 8 = 40 slices are left   **b.** 14 × 16 = 224 slices of bread

Page 9:
a. 420 bags   **b.** 770 bags

Page 11:
a. 12 × $0.05 = $0.60   **b.** 20 × $0.05 = $1.00   **c.** 45 × $0.05 = $2.25
d. 36 × $0.05 = $1.80

Page 16:
a. $\frac{1}{2} \times 16$ **b.** 8 cups of flour   **c.** $\frac{1}{4} \times 24$ **d.** 6 cups of water

Page 20:
a. 11 cups bread flour, 2 tablespoons (T.) salt, 5 T. rapid rise yeast,
   32 ounces very warm water, 2 T. olive oil, 4 T. honey
b. 56

Page 23:
b. (4 × 3) + 1   **c.** (2 × 5) + 3
   4 × 3 = 12   2 × 5 = 10
   12 + 1 = 13   10 + 3 = 13

Page 25:
a. The restaurant owner needs to serve 60 customers.
       8 × 8 = 64
   She would need to buy 8 packets of tortillas to feed 60 people.
b. She would have 4 remainder tortillas.

Page 27:
a. 3,000 ÷ 100 = 30   **b.** 20 × 100 = 2,000   **c.** 52 × 10 = 520
d. 1,000 ÷ 10 = 100

Problem-Solving Activity

Step 1: 150 cupcakes ÷ 25 cupcakes per batch = 6 batches
Step 2: 150 cupcakes ÷ 4 cupcakes per tray = 37 trays and 2 remainder cupcakes
Step 3:
$$\begin{array}{r} 37 \text{ R } ②\\ 4\overline{)150} \\ -148 \\ \hline 2 \end{array}$$
$= 37\frac{2}{4}$

Step 4: $2.00 × 37 = $74.00